Ultimate Italy And Rome Trivia

Interesting Facts About Italy And
Hundreds Of Challenging Italy And
Rome Trivia To Try

Miller D. Claire

Table Of Contents

INTRODUCTION.......................................5

Chapter 1: Interesting Facts About Italy.........8

Chapter 2: Italy General Knowledge Trivia Questions...25

Chapter 3: Italy Multiple Choice Trivia Questions And Answers....................................31

Chapter 4: Italy Geography Trivia Questions And Answers...40

Chapter 5: Italian History Trivia Questions And Answers...43

Chapter 6: Italian Food Trivia Questions And Answers...47

Chapter 7: Italian Art Trivia Questions And Answers...50

Chapter 8: Italian Music Trivia Questions And Answers...54

Chapter 9: Italian Sports Trivia Questions And Answers...57

Chapter 10; Italian Literature Trivia Questions And Answers...60

Chapter 11: Italian Movies & TV Shows Trivia Questions And Answers...62

Chapter 12: Italian Language Trivia Questions And Answers..................65

Chapter 13: Italian Famous Landmarks Trivia Questions And Answers..................68

Chapter 14: Rome General Knowledge Trivia Questions And Answers..................71

Chapter 15: Rome Multiple Choice Trivia Questions And Answers..................74

Chapter 16: Roman Movies & TV Shows Trivia Questions And Answers..................79

Chapter 17: History of Rome Trivia Questions And Answers..................82

Chapter 18: Roman Empire Trivia Questions And Answers..................85

Chapter 19: Rome Music Trivia Questions And Answers..................88

Chapter 20: Rome Sport Trivia Questions And Answers..................91

Chapter 21: Rome True or False Trivia Questions And Answers..................94

Chapter 22: Rome Travel Trivia Questions And Answers..................97

Photographs Of Some Top Attractions In Italy

ITALY

INTRODUCTION

Italy is a country in Europe that looks like a boot when you see it on a map. It's famous for its delicious food, like pizza and pasta, and its beautiful cities, like Rome, Venice, and Florence. Italy has lots of history, with ancient ruins from the Roman Empire, like the Colosseum and the Forum. People in Italy speak Italian, and they love to enjoy life with good food, music, and art. The countryside is also very pretty, with rolling hills, vineyards, and olive groves. Whether you're exploring the bustling streets of Rome or relaxing by the colorful houses in Cinque Terre, Italy has something for everyone to enjoy. Let's explore Italy in more detail:

Cities: Italy has many famous cities. Rome is the capital and has ancient ruins like the Colosseum and the Roman Forum. Venice is known for its canals where people ride in boats called gondolas. Florence is famous for its art, including the statue of David by

Michelangelo. Milan is a big fashion city where designers make stylish clothes.

Food: Italian food is loved all over the world. Pizza, with its thin crust and tasty toppings, originally comes from Italy. Pasta, like spaghetti and lasagna, is also popular. Italians use fresh ingredients like tomatoes, olive oil, and cheese to make their dishes extra delicious.

History: Italy has a long history. In ancient times, it was home to powerful empires like Rome. The Roman Empire built impressive structures like the Colosseum and aqueducts. Italy was also the birthplace of the Renaissance, a time of great art and learning.

Landscapes: Italy has diverse landscapes. It has beautiful beaches along the Mediterranean Sea where people swim and relax in the sun. In the north, there are tall mountains like the Alps, where people go skiing in the winter.

Culture: Italians are known for their passion for life. They enjoy spending time with family and friends, eating good food, and celebrating festivals. Italian music, like opera, is famous around the world, and Italian fashion is admired for its style and elegance.

Chapter 1: Interesting Facts About Italy

- Italy is larger than Arizona.
- In Italy, twenty percent or so of the population is over 65.

- Italy is bordered by Austria, France, Vatican City, San Marino, Slovenia, and Switzerland.

- The longest border is that with Switzerland.

- The average Italian household has 1.27 children.

- All people above the age of 18 are eligible to vote, but to participate in a Senate election, a candidate must be at least 25.

- Among the newest countries in Western Europe is Italy.

- Italy has more World Heritage sites than any other country.

- Rome is more than two thousand years old.

- The country was ruled by a dictatorship for twenty years.

- Cats are treasured and sought after in Italy.
- Italy is home to the oldest university in Europe.
- In Italy, police use Lamborghinis.
- There are just twenty-one letters in the Italian alphabet.
- Twelve minority languages are recognized by law in Italy.
- Italy is the world's supplier of olive oil.
- The last Italian king ruled for a mere thirty-six days.
- The Italian flag was modeled after the French banner used during Napoleon's invasion of the Italian Peninsula in 1797.
- The typical Italian makes $26,700 a year, although those who reside in

the affluent north earn close to $40,000.

- Italy is bordered to the north by France, Switzerland, Austria, and Slovenia and is surrounded by the Mediterranean, Tyrrhenian, Ionian, and Adriatic seas.
- The Mafia is still in operation in Italy.
- Pinocchio was initially published in an Italian newspaper.
- Italy may have more than 1500 lakes.
- Italy's highest summit is Mont Blanc.
- Italy is home to the three active volcanoes in Europe.
- Italy is home to the thermometer's inventor.
- About 8.6% of Italians are unemployed, but in the country's

more impoverished south, that number can rise to 20%.

- The Sistine Chapel welcomes around 20,000 visitors each day.
- Tourists throw €1,000,000 into the Trevi Fountain annually.
- Italian farms produce potatoes, sugar beets, soybeans, wheat, olives, meat, and dairy goods.
- The average life expectancy of an Italian is 79.54 years at birth.
- The well-known children's book Pinocchio was written by an Italian.
- The city of Naples is where pizza first appeared.
- Italy is where the piano originated.
- The invention of batteries originated in Italy.
- Columbus himself was of Italian heritage.

- The first bank was founded in Italy.
- Italians invented glassware.
- The Po is the longest river in Italy.
- The average Italian consumes half a pound of bread per day.
- Italian science is credited with creating the electric battery, wireless telegraphy, nitroglycerin, and barometer, among other things.
- Famous Italian explorers include Christopher Columbus, Marco Polo, John Cabot, and Amerigo Vespucci.

- The current Italian language originated in the Tuscany region.
- The nuclear reactor is credited to Enrico Fermi, an Italian.
- One of the most well-known products made in Italy is the Fiat car.

- With over 40 million visitors, Italy ranks as the fourth most visited nation worldwide.
- There are two microstates in Italy: San Marino and Vatican City.
- Shakespeare's plays that are either entirely or partially set in Italy include Julius Caesar, Romeo and Juliet, Othello, The Merchant of Venice, Antony and Cleopatra, Coriolanus, Cymbeline, Much Ado About Nothing, Othello, The Taming of the Shrew, Titus Andronicus, The Two Gentlemen of Verona, and The Winter's Tale.
- It is Italy that produces cologne.
- The ice cream cone was created by Italians.
- The main places from which Italian immigrants came to the United

States were Naples and southern Italy.

- Pompeii, an ancient city, was destroyed by the active volcano Mount Vesuvius.
- The last eruption of Mount Vesuvius occurred in 1944, destroying numerous nearby communities.
- The Italians are credited with creating spectacles.
- The average age of an Italian is 41 years old.
- Italy is divided into 16 regions and 4 autonomous regions.
- Before the country adopted the euro, its currency was the Italian lira.
- The average Italian consumes 26 liters of wine per year.

- Italy's principal industries include tourism, machinery, iron and steel, chemicals, food processing, textiles, cars, clothing, footwear, and ceramics.
- Italy has more hotel rooms than any other European nation.
- Italy is credited with creating the espresso machine.
- Italy has the world's fifth-largest industrial economy.
- Just over one-third of Italy's land is arable and suitable for cultivation.
- Italy's principal trading partners are the US, the UK, Germany, and France.
- In Italy, about 40% of laborers are union members.
- The telephone was invented by an Italian (Meucci).

- The northern cities of Milan, Turin, and Genoa are the hubs of most of Italy's industrial activity.
- Italy has had approximately sixty different governments since the end of World War II.
- Europe's wealthiest region is the area surrounding Venice.
- More than 75% of Italy is hilly or mountainous.
- Italy is credited with developing the typewriter.
- Though Italy today has the lowest birthrate in Europe, Italians were historically known for having large families.
- A considerable percentage of Italy's prosperity can be ascribed to hundreds of tiny, privately owned firms.

- Italian families save three times more money than American families, as well as more than German and Japanese families.
- A typical Italian eats twenty-five kg of pasta annually.
- With a population of almost 5 million, Rome is the biggest city in Italy.
- Italy is home to more than 58 million people.
- Italians refer to their country as Italia.
- Italy imports more than 75% of its energy.
- The service sector accounts for over 70% of the Italian economy.
- Agriculture used to account for more than one-third of Italy's GDP.

Right now, it is less than three percent.

- Italian is the official language, while some people also speak French and German.
- The summers are warm and the winters are crisp in northern Italy. Warm summers and mild winters are common in South Italy.
- The Seven Hills of Rome are Aventine, Caelian, Capitoline, Esquiline, Palatine, Quirinal, and Viminal.
- The SPQR mark is seen on many ancient buildings in Rome. As such, it stands for "the people and senate of Rome."
- Rome was founded in 753 BC.
- It took until 1861 for Italy to coalesce as a nation.

- Italy's national protest song is Bella Ciao. It was made popular by Italian partisans during World War II and is a prominent sound at protests.
- Before Rome became a republic and then an empire, it was ruled by seven kings.
- Rome's first monarch was none other than Romulus, the mythical city's founder.
- In Italian, the saying "Ars longa, vita brevis" is frequently cited. Its meaning—"Art is long, life is short"—captures the Italian love of leisure.
- The Cloacus Maxima sewer system in Rome is a wonder of ancient engineering.

- Augustus Octavian became the first Roman Emperor, ascending to the throne in 27 BC.

- The Roman Empire fell in 476 AD when barbarian invaders forced the last Roman emperor, Romulus Augustulus, to resign.

- A centurion commanded a hundred thousand men.

- A legion in Rome numbered six thousand troops.

- Italy is home to 1.27 million international residents.

- Italy's present constitution went into effect on January 1, 1948.

- The president of Italy is a ceremonial figure.

- The person in charge of the government and the country is the prime minister.

- Inno di Mameli has been Italy's national song since October 1946.
- Green, white, and red make up the Italian flag.
- Three virtues are represented by the colors of the Italian flag: charity (crimson), hope (green), and faith (white).
- While it lacks an official slogan, the Italian Republic frequently uses the statement "L'Italia e' una Repubblica democratica, fondata sul lavoro" (Italy is a democratic Republic, based on labor).
- Italy's patron saint is Saint. Francis of Assisi and Saint. Caterina of Siena.
- Italy has a 98% Roman Catholic population.

- Italy is home to the Roman Catholic Church.
- Italy is home to about 3,000 museums.
- Soccer, sometimes referred to as football outside of America, is the national sport of Italy.
- Pasta is the national dish of Italy.
- Latin, the language of the Roman Empire, gave rise to Italian.
- The Adriatic, Ionian, Tyrrhenean, Ligurian, and Mediterranean seas are around the Italian peninsula.
- There are several smaller islands in Italy, but Sicily and Sardinia are the two biggest.

- The Italian island of Sicily is home to the infamous Mafia criminal organization.
- Napoleon's first exile took place on the Italian island of Elba.
- The Alps mountain range, which forms part of Italy's northern border, has historically protected the peninsula against foreign invasion.
- Three active volcanoes are located in Italy: Stromboli, Etna, and Vesuvius.
- Naples is the largest city in southern Italy.
- After Rome, Milan is the second-largest city in Italy.
- Milan is the hub of Italian fashion and finance.
- Rome is known to us as "The Eternal City."

- Florence is the home of Italian art.

- Vespas are motor scooters that are commonly used for transportation in congested city streets. They are manufactured in Italy.

Chapter 2: Italy General Knowledge Trivia Questions

Discover a treasure trove of Italian and Roman trivia questions & answers that will transport you to the heart of Italy's bella vita, a land of history and romance with iconic cities, stunning coastlines, and a culinary heritage that is second to none and its capital.

Now take out your pen and paper, and let's get started with these fantastic Italy and Rome quiz questions and answers!

Remember, every Question Is A Jig Of Knowledge!!

<u>**Questions;**</u>

1. What is the capital of Italy?

2. What colors does the Italian flag consist of?

3. Which currency is in circulation in Italy?

4. What century was the unification of Italy?

5. Who was Italy's last king?

6. What shape is similar to Italy's?

7. What is Italy's official name?

8. Which nations—aside from enclaves—share a geographical boundary with Italy?

9. Italy is home to enclaves of two nations. Which are they?

10. How many official languages are there in Italy?

11. Who is the Italian astronomer known for his discoveries supporting the heliocentric theory?

12. Which cities do the words "planes", "more" and "testier" represent?

13. Which Tuscan city on the Arno can you visit Michelangelo's "David," Leonardo da Vinci's "Annunciation," and the Duomo via Bird scooters

14. Who is often referred to as the patron saint of Italy?

Answers;

1. Rome

2. Green, White, and Red

3. Euro

4. 19th century

5. Umberto II

6. A boot

7. Repubblica Italiana (Italian Republic)

8. 4. Switzerland, France, Slovenia and Austria.

9. San Marino and Vatican City

10.   One is Italian.

11.   Galileo Galilei.

12.   Naples, Rome, Trieste

13.   Florence

14.   Saint Francis of Assisi.

Chapter 3: Italy Multiple Choice Trivia Questions And Answers

<u>Questions;</u>

1. When did the ashes of Mount Vesuvius destroy Pompeii?
   29AD
   79AD
   159AD
   189AD

2. Which river is the longest in Italy?
   River Po
   River Adige
   River Piave
   River Tiber

3. What is the name of Rome's only one sister?
   New York City

Madrid

Paris

Berlin

4. Where in Italy was Shakespeare's "Romeo and Juliet" set?
Rome
Verona
Bologna
Florence

5. One town is part of Amalfi Coast, which is it?
Positano
Vernazza
Lecce
Burano

6. There is a city in Italy known for its Neapolitan cuisine, which city is it?
Naples

Rome
Palermo
Bari

7. Italy was reckoned with a political scandal in the 1990s, what was the name?
Clean Feet
Dirty Feet
Dirty Hands
Clean Hands

8. Italy has what kind of government?
Hereditary Monarchy
Guerilla
No Government
Republic

9. What is the name of the Italian city with a larger population?
Verona

Naples

Catania

Rome

10. Italy totally surrounded which country?
San Marino
Monaco
Malta
Corsica

11. The highest geographical point in Italy is called what?
Mount Katahdin
Mount Everest
Mount Rushmore
Mont Blanc

12. What is the name of the European lake located in Italy?
Lake Bracciano

Lake Drawsko

Lake Burtnieks

Lake Goplo

13.   Which sport did Italy win the World Cup in 2006?
Golf

Soccer

Rowing

Hockey

14.   Among the following, which of them is an island in Italy?
Morocco

Mykonos

Nantucket

Sicily

15.   One of these luxury brands is headquartered in Rome, Italy, which is it?

Ralph Lauren
Bulgari (BVLGARI)
Adolfo Dominguez
Stradivarius

16. What do red flowers represent in
Italy?
Rage
Open Passion
Jealousy
Secrecy

17. What does a gift of yellow flowers
suggest in Italy?
Jealousy
Romance
Bad Luck
Hatred

18.   What is the name of the Italian explorer who explored the Mississippi Valley in America?

Marco Polo

Christopher Columbus

James Madsen

Henri De Tonti

<u>Answers;</u>

1. 79AD
2. River Po
3. Paris
4. Verona
5. Positano
6. Naples
7. Clean hands
8. Republic
9. Rome
10. San Marino
11. Mont Blanc
12. Lake Bracciano
13. Soccer
14. Sicily
15. Bulgari
16. Secrecy
17. Jealousy
18. Henri De Tonti

Chapter 4: Italy Geography Trivia Questions And Answers

<u>Questions;</u>

1. The town of Alghero is found on which island?

2. The capital of Sicily is what?

3. Which range of mountains can you find at the border between Italy and France, which range of mountains can you find there?

4. Capital of Puglia is what?

5. In the northern Italian Alps, which UNESCO site is made of 18 peaks?

6. Naples is the capital of what region?

7. In Northern Italy, which UNESCO site is made of 5 seaside Villages?

8. Which lake is the largest in Italy?

9. A river flows through Rome, which is it?

10. Where will you find Spiaggia dei Conigli?

11. Which mountain range forms Italy's northern border?

12. What is the name of the Italian island in the Tyrrhenian Sea that is famous for its blue grottoes?

<u>**Answers;**</u>

1. Sardinia
2. Palermo
3. The Alps
4. Bari
5. The Dolomites
6. Campania
7. Cinque Terre
8. Lake Garda
9. River Tiber
10. Lampedusa
11. The Alps.
12. Capri

Chapter 5: Italian History Trivia Questions And Answers

<u>Questions;</u>

1. Christopher Columbus was born where?

2. The first emperor of Rome is who?

3. Which republic was Lorenzo de Medici de facto ruler?

4. Italy's first capital is what?

5. Italy became a republic in what year?

6. Prime Minister was elected in 2001, who was he?

7. In the 16th century, an Italian noblewoman became queen of France, who was she?

8. Which year did Italy enter WWI?

9. The National Fascist Party was founded by which politician?

10. In February 2021, who was the prime minister?

11. What traditional Italian celebration takes place on December 24th and features a feast of seven different fish dishes?

12. Who founded modern nursing practices and is referred to as the lady with the lamp?

13. What is the name of the Italian scientist who invented the battery and made significant contributions to electricity?

<u>Answers;</u>

1. Genoa
2. Augustus Caesar
3. Republic of Florence
4. Turin
5. 1946
6. Silvio Berlusconi
7. Catherine de Medici
8. 1915
9. Benito Mussolini
10. Mario Draghi
11. La Vigilia (Christmas Eve dinner).
12. Florence Nightingale (who had Italian heritage).
13. Alessandro Volta.

Chapter 6: Italian Food Trivia Questions And Answers

<u>Questions;</u>

1. Pizza was invented in which Italian city?

2. A typical Sicilian dish made of a stuffed rice ball is called what?

3. What is the of the milk used in making traditional mozzarella?

4. The cut of meat used in an Osso Bucco, what is the name?

5. Pasta Carbonara was invented in which city?

6. Focaccia is which type of food?

7. The Italian dessert can be translated as "lift me up" is what?

8. The main ingredient in the sauce of a Risotto ai Funghi is what?

9. Parmigiano belongs to which cheese family?

10. In Italy, a dish consists of slices of raw beef sprinkled with oil and Parmesan cheese which is it?

11. What is the name of the Italian dessert that is made of fried dough dusted with powdered sugar?

12. What is the name of the Italian dish made of thinly sliced eggplant that is layered with tomato sauce and cheese?

<u>**Answers;**</u>

1. Naples
2. Arancini
3. Buffalo's milk
4. Veal shanks
5. Rome
6. Bread
7. Tiramisu
8. Mushrooms
9. Grana
10. Carpaccio
11. Zeppole
12. Eggplant Parmesan (Melanzane alla Parmigiana).

Chapter 7: Italian Art Trivia Questions And Answers

<u>**Questions;**</u>

1. The Last Supper was painted by who?

2. The frescoes were painted on the ceiling of the Sistine Chapel by who?

3. At Florence's Galleria dell'Accademia, which famous statue can you find there?

4. "The Birth of Venus" by Sandro Botticelli can be found in which museum?

5. "The School of Athens" was painted by who?

6. The Botticelli painting that can be translated from Italian to "Spring" is what?

7. The Italian artist whose real name was "Michelangelo Merisi" us who?

8. The Feast of Herod and Lo Zuccone was made by which Italian sculptor?

9. Uffizi Gallery is found in which Italian city?

10. The mentor of Michelangelo is which family?

11. Which Italian Renaissance artist painted the Mona Lisa?

12.   What is the Italian word used for "beautiful" often used to compliment art and scenery?

<u>Answers;</u>

1. Leonardo da Vinci
2. Michelangelo
3. David
4. Uffizi Gallery in Florence
5. Rafael
6. Primavera
7. Caravaggio
8. Donatello
9. Florence
10. Medici family
11. Leonardo da Vinci.
12. Bello

Chapter 8: Italian Music Trivia Questions And Answers

<u>Questions;</u>

1. "La Boheme" opera was written by who?

2. "La solitudine" was sung by who?

3. "Fall on Me" was sung by which Italian tenor?

4. "Ti Amo" was sang by who?

5. "Lasciatemi cantare" was sang by who?

6. Eros Ramazzotti released his first album when?

7. The "Rigoletto" opera was written by who?

8. The Milan Theatre known for its operas, ballets, and concerts in the entire world is what?

9. The Italian term that describes the fact of singing without instrumental accompaniment is what?

10. The national anthem of Italy is what?

11. What is the traditional Italian stringed instrument similar to a guitar?

<u>Answers;</u>

1. Puccini
2. Laura Pausini
3. Andrea Bocelli
4. Umberto Tozzi
5. Toto Cutugno
6. 80s
7. Giuseppe Verdi
8. Teatro della Scala
9. A cappella
10. Il canto degli italiani
11. The mandolin.

Chapter 9: Italian Sports Trivia Questions And Answers

<u>Questions;</u>

1. What is the Italian word for "football" (soccer)?

2. which race is the Palio in Sienna?

3. Italy won the football world cup how many times?

4. The Argentinian footballer who used to play for Napoli in the 80s was who?

5. The two main football teams in Rome are what?

6. The 2006 Winter Olympics was hosted in which Italian city?

7. The Italian Open was held in which Italian city?

8. Italy was part of which European Rugby competition

9. What does "Calcio" mean in Italy?

10. Valentina Marchei is known for which sport?

11. Who was the constructor that got the most wins at the Italian Grand Prix?

1. Calcio
2. Horse race
3. 4 times (1934, 1938, 1982 and 2006)
4. Diego Maradona
5. SS Lazio and AS Roma
6. Turin
7. Rome
8. Six Nations
9. Football
10. Figure skating
11. Ferrari

Chapter 10; Italian Literature Trivia Questions And Answers

Questions;

1. "Machiavellian" is a term given to which author?

2. "If this is a man" was written by who?

3. Divine Comedy was written by which Italian poet?

4. "The Name of the Rose" was written by who?

5. Frances Mayes's book adapted into a movie in 2003 is what?

<u>Answers;</u>

1. Niccolò di Bernardo dei Machiavelli
2. Primo Michele Levi
3. Dante
4. Umberto Eco
5. Under the Tuscan sun

Chapter 11: Italian Movies & TV Shows Trivia Questions And Answers

1. Anita Ekberg in the Trevi Fountain is seen in which movie?

2. Audrey Hepburn and Gregory Peck started in which movie in Italy?

3. A sequel to The Da Vinci Code, was partially filmed in Rome, which movie is it?

4. The Marriage Italian Style movie was directed by who?

5. Dickie Greenleaf in The Talented Mr. Ripley was played by who?

6. Audrey Hepburn starred as a princess in which 1953 movie?

7. Elizabeth Gilbert in Eat Pray Love was played by who?

8. The 2021 Disney movie that was set in the Cinque Terre is what?

9. Michael Corleone in The Godfather was played by who?

10.   The teen movie that was set in Rome and stars Hilary Duff is what?

<u>**Answers;**</u>

1. La Dolce Vita

2. Roman Holiday

3. Angels and Demons

4. Vittorio De Sica

5. Jude Law

6. Roman Holiday

7. Julia Roberts

8. Luca

9. Al Pacino

10. Lizzie McGuire the movie

Chapter 12: Italian Language Trivia Questions And Answers

1. The English equivalent of "In bocca al lupo" is what?

2. What is "Buon compleanno"?

3. What is "Prego"?

4. What does "Come stai" mean?

5. What does "la colazione" mean?

6. What does "cornetto" mean?

7. What does "succo di frutta" mean?

8. What is "cold" in the Italian language?

9. The letter used at the end of a feminine word is what?

10. What is "to eat" in the Italian language?

<u>**Answers;**</u>

1. Break a leg (good luck)
2. Happy Birthday
3. You're welcome
4. How are you
5. Breakfast
6. A croissant
7. Fruit juice
8. Freddo
9. A
10. Mangiare

Chapter 13: Italian Famous Landmarks Trivia Questions And Answers

Questions:

1. Papal basilica in Vatican City is what?

2. Rialto Bridge (Ponte di Rialto) can be found in which Italian city?

3. Which city can you find 30% of UNESCO's important works of art?

4. Leaning tower of Pisa is which sort of tower?

5. Blue Grotto is found on which island?

6. Galleria Vittorio Emanuele II is in which Italian city?

7. The train that goes from Naples to Sorrento, through Pompeii is called what?

8. The pink beach of Budelli is found in which archipelago?

9. The Star of the Turks (Scala dei Turchi) is found on which island?

10. Trulli houses are found in which region?

11. Which Italian car manufacturer produced models like the 488 GTB and the Portofino?

12. The famous tower in Venice that leans to one side, what is its name?

<u>**Answers;**</u>

1. St. Peter's Basilica
2. Venice
3. Florence
4. Campanile of the Cathedral of Pisa
5. Capri island
6. Milan
7. Circumvesuviana
8. La Maddalena
9. Sicily
10. Puglia
11. Ferrari
12. Campanile di San Marco (St. Mark's Campanile).

Chapter 14: Rome General Knowledge Trivia Questions And Answers

Questions:

1. Within the city of Rome, which independent city lies there?

2. What does "The Senate and People of Rome" represent?

3. Romulus found Rome when?

4. Which of the Italian rivers flows through Rome?

5. Rome's most popular nickname is what?

6. The capital of Italy before Rome is what?

7. The biggest university in Rome is what?

8. Rome was built on how many hills?

9. Rome is the capital of which Italian region?

<u>**Answers;**</u>

1. Vatican City.
2. SPQR
3. 753 BC.
4. River Tiber
5. The Eternal City.
6. Florence.
7. La Sapienza University.
8. Seven.
9. Lazio

Chapter 15: Rome Multiple Choice Trivia Questions And Answers

1. In Italy, which animals are free to move about?
   Dogs
   Cats
   Snakes
   Foxes

2. What is the estimated amount of money that is tossed in the Trevi Fountain every day?
   1,000 euros
   2,000 euros
   3,000 euros
   4,000 euros

3. The coins collected in the Trevi Fountain are donated where?
   Cancer Charity

Susan G. Komen for the Cure
Catholic Charity and Caritas
SOME

4. Rome has how many fountains?
   1500
   1800
   2000
   3500

5. What is the name of the largest Vatican church in the world?
   St Peter's Basilica
   Santa Maria
   Basilica of Saint Paul
   All Saints Anglican Church

6. Rome has how many churches?
   500
   600
   700

900

7. What is Rome's size in square kilometers?
685 Square Km
885 Square Km
1,085 Square Km
1,285 Square Km

8. When was Great Fire of Rome?
BC 64
BC 24
AD 24
AD 64

9. What does Ponentino mean?
A wind
A pasta dish
A drink
A river

10.   Rome has how many districts?

14

18

22

16

<u>Answers;</u>

1. Cats

2. 3,000 euros

3. Catholic Charity and Caritas

4. 2000

5. St Peter's Basilica

6. 900

7. 1,285 Square km.

8. AD 64

9. A wind.

10.   22

Chapter 16: Roman Movies & TV Shows Trivia Questions And Answers

1. Ben Stiller directed which movie in 2016?

2. The role of Princess Anne in Roman Holiday was played by who?

3. Roman actors were called?

4. The role of charming sociopath Tom Ripley in The Talented Mr. Ripley was played by who?

5. Rome movies won many Oscars?

6. The 2012 Romance/Comedy film To Rome With Love was directed by who?

7. At the beginning of the movie, Angels & Demons someone died in the Vatican, who was the person?

8. Marisa Tomei played a role in "Only You", a romantic drama directed by Harry Wootliff, what is the name of the role?

9. Anita Ekberg swam in the Trevi Fountain in which movie?

10. The name of Julia Robert's character in Eat Pray Love was what?

<u>**Answers;**</u>

1. Zoolander 2.

2. Audrey Hepburn.

3. Histriones.

4. Matt Damon.

5. Three.

6. Woody Allen.

7. The Pope.

8. Faith.

9. La dolce vita.

10. Elizabeth Gilbert

Chapter 17: History of Rome Trivia Questions And Answers

1. Remus and Romulus are found on which hill?

2. Remus and Romulus were nursed by which creature?

3. When did Rome finally destroy Carthage (in the Third Punic War)?

4. What is the name of the Roman city that was buried and destroyed during the volcanic eruption of Mount Vesuvius in 79 A.D?

5. The tribe that successfully invaded Italy, which included the sacking of Rome in 410 was what?

6. The former Roman temple, now a Catholic church built by Marcus Agrippa is what?

7. The person allowed to wear togas in Ancient Rome was who?

8. while Rome burned to the ground during the Great Fire of Rome, which Roman emperor was singing and dancing the fiddle?

9. Rome's port city until the 4th century A.D. was called what?

10. Construction of the Aurelian Wall was started by who?

Answers;

1. Palatine Hill
2. She-wolf
3. 146 BC.
4. Pompeii.
5. Visigoths.
6. Pantheon.
7. Only free-born Men.
8. Emperor Nero.
9. Ostia Antica.
10. Emperor Aurelian

Chapter 18: Roman Empire Trivia Questions And Answers

<u>**Questions;**</u>

1. The famous Roman general who conquered Gaul was who?

2. The First Triumvirate in 60 BC was formed by who?

3. Christianity is the official religion of the empire that was made by which emperor?

4. The capital of the Roman Empire was moved to the city of Byzantium in 330 CE by who?

5. The leader of the military forces of Carthage that fought against Rome in the Second Punic War was who?

6. What was the name of the first king of Rome?

7. What was the name of the first Emperor of the Roman Empire?

8. What is the name of the Egyptian ruler who was Julius Caesar's lover?

9. What does "I came, I saw, I conquered" represents in Latin?

10. Julius Agricola defeated the Caledonii in A.D. 83 in which battle?

<u>Answers;</u>

1. Gaius Julius Caesar
2. Pompeii
3. Emperor Theodosius.
4. Constantine the Great.
5. Hannibal Barca.
6. Romulus
7. Augustus.
8. Cleopatra
9. Veni vidi vici
10. Mons Graupius.

Chapter 19: Rome Music Trivia Questions And Answers

1. AS Roma football club anthem was sung by who?

2. Claudio Baglioni stayed in the charts for 27 weeks in which Album?

3. What is the name of the artist from Rome who has studied at the European Academy of Dramatic Art and starred in the film Pazze di Me?

4. Ennio Morricone won his first Oscars when?

5. Rock in Roma 2019 music festival was held where in Rome?

6. Someone won Italy's most prestigious award, the Targa Tenco, with his self-titled debut album in 1994, what is the name of the person?

7. Who sang Per un Bacio (For a Kiss) and La Matrona (The Matron)?

8. What is the name of the person who always organizes the Roma Jazz Festival in Rome?

9. What is the name of the Rome-born singer that sang 'Grazie Roma'?

10. What is the name of the Roman singer who released an album called 'The Space Between' in 2007?

<u>Answers;</u>

1. Antonello Venditti.
2. La Vita é Adesso.
3. Margherita Vicario.
4. 2016.
5. Capannelle Racecourse.
6. Daniele Silvestri.
7. Margherita Vicario.
8. International Music Festival Foundation (IMF).
9. Antonello Venditti
10. Chiara Civello

Chapter 20: Rome Sport Trivia Questions And Answers

1. The two football teams in Rome are called what?

2. What are the names of the athletes who competed in sports in ancient Rome?

3. Chariot races held in ancient Rome were done where?

4. What was the name of the most famous Roman chariot racer?

5. The sports facility that hosted the Coppa Italia was called what?

6. Rome holds the Summer Olympics in which year?

7. Who won the Rally Di Roma Capitale in 2019?

8. The horses that pulled a Roman chariot, how many were they?

9. What is the name of the person who used to fight in the Colosseum?

10.   The Giro d'Italia grand finale was held in Rome which year?

<u>**Answers;**</u>

1. A.S. Roma and Lazio
2. Slaves, Criminals, and prisoners.
3. Circus Maximus.
4. Gaius Appuleius Diocles.
5. Stadio Olimpico
6. 1960
7. Giandomenico Basso.
8. Four.
9. Gladiators.
10. 2018.

Chapter 21: Rome True or False Trivia Questions And Answers

1. Is it true that the population of Rome is under 2 million inhabitants?

2. Is it true that the President of the Republic of Italy resides in the Quirinal Palace?

3. Is it true that the Trastevere is located south of the Vatican?

4. Is it true that the Ampo de' Fiori is an urban park in Rome?

5. Is it true that Rome has more than 900 churches?

6. Is it true that Rome is the economic centre of Italy?

7. Is it true that Rome was the last city-state to become part of a unified?

8. It's said that Romulus killed his twin brother, Remus, is it true?

9. Is it true that the Spanish Steps are actually French?

10. Is it fair enough to say that there are more inhabitants in Rome than in Madrid?

1. False
2. True
3. True
4. False
5. True
6. False
7. True
8. True
9. True
10. False

Chapter 22: Rome Travel Trivia Questions And Answers

1. The main street that runs from Piazza del Popolo to Piazza Venezia is called what?

2. The steps on Piazza di Spagna are called what?

3. Michelangelo painted which chapel's ceiling?

4. Rome has how many airports?

5. Colosseum is on which metro line?

6. What is the name of the largest station in Rome?

7. What is the name of the piazza where you can find a monument that honors the first king of Italy?

8. What are the names of the rivers that are represented on the Fontana dei Quattro Fiumi?

9. The passage that connects the Vatican to Castel Sant'Angelo is called what?

10. The public transport company that operates most of the public transport lines in Rome is called what?

1. Via del Corso
2. Spanish Steps
3. Sistine Chapel
4. Two.
5. blue
6. Roma Termini
7. Piazza Venezia
8. The Nile, the Danube, the Ganges, and the Río de la Plata.
9. The Passetto di Borgo
10. ATAC

<u>Photographs Of Some Top Attractions In Italy</u>

- **Leaning Tower**

- **Lake Como**

- ## Pompeii

- **Colosseum**

- **Pantheon**

● Grand Canal

- **Santa Maria del Fiore.**

● St. Peter's Basilica

• Capri

- **Mount Etna**

● Dolomites

● Santa Maria delle Grazie

- ## **Trevi Fountain**

- **Verona Arena**